Mapping Earthforms

W9-BBC-427

Deserts

Catherine Chambers

Heinemann Library

Designed by David Oakley
Illustrations by Tokay Interactive
Originated by Dot Gradations
Printed in China

09 08 07 06
10 9 8 7 6 5 4 3

Library of Congress Cataloging-in-Publication Data
Chambers, Catherine, 1954-
    Deserts / Catherine Chambers.
        p. cm. – (Mapping earthforms)
    Includes bibliographical references (p.) and index.
    Summary: Explores the world's deserts, discussing how they were formed, what
organisms live there, and how they are used by humans.
    ISBN 1-57572-522-3 (lib. bdg.)   ISBN 1-4034-0032-6 (pbk. bdg.)
        1. Deserts—Juvenile literature. [1. Deserts.] I. Title.
GB612.C48 2000
508.15'421—dc21
                            99-043375

Acknowledgments
The Publishers would like to thank the following for permission to reproduce photographs: Still
Pictures/S. Pern, p. 4; Still Pictures/W. Fautre, p. 5; Robert Harding Picture Library/J. Greenberg, p.
7; G. R. Roberts, pp. 8, 10, 24; Oxford Scientific Films/K. Atkinson, p. 9; Oxford Scientific Films/R.
Packwood, p. 11; Oxford Scientific Films/M. Brown, p. 12; Still Pictures/M. Denis-Hoot, p. 13;
Anthony King, p. 15; Oxford Scientific Films/F. Ehrenstrom, p. 17; Oxford Scientific Films/J. Foote,
p. 18; Oxford Scientific Films/C. Monteath, p. 19; Still Pictures/UNEP, p. 20; Still Pictures/H.
Schwarzbach, p. 22; Still Pictures, p. 23; Robert Harding Picture Library/ R. Ashworth, p. 25; Still
Pictures/R. Buttiker, p. 26; Ecoscene/R. Hughes, p. 27; Still Pictures/G. Wiltsie, p. 29.

Cover photograph reproduced with permission of Bruce Coleman Limited.

Every effort has been made to contact copyright holders of any material reproduced in this
book. Any omissions will be rectified in subsequent printings if notice is given to the publisher.

Some words are shown in bold, **like this.**
You can find out what they mean by looking in the glossary.

Contents

What Is a Desert?

Most deserts are huge areas of very dry land. Some deserts are frozen. Many deserts are so dry or frozen that few plants are able to grow. Deserts receive less than 10 inches (25 centimeters) of rain each year. Sometimes there is no rain at all.

There are hot, cold, and frozen deserts. Deserts on high **plateaus**, where the air is cooler, are called cold deserts, but they are often very hot during the day. In the **polar regions**, deserts are frozen all year. At night, hot, cold, and frozen deserts are all very cold.

How did deserts begin?

Some deserts began thousands of years ago. Others have existed for not much more than 1,000 years. The hot **climate** in some

The Gobi is a cold desert that lies on a plateau in central Asia. It has rolling hills covered in small stones. Some deserts have a covering of volcanic gravel.

The Sahara is a hot desert covering much of northern Africa. Just over 8,000 years ago, it was green and **fertile.** There are signs that ancient river valleys were once part of what is now dry desert.

parts of the world dried up the land. In this book, we will find out how today's climate keeps the deserts dry. We will also discover how people cause some desert areas to spread.

What do deserts look like?

Some deserts are very rocky, while others are covered with stones or gravel. Some are vast stretches of fine sand, while others are large areas of ice.

High winds and hard rain have turned desert rocks and sand into unusual shapes. We will discover how different types of deserts are made and how the shapes are formed.

Life in the desert

Many deserts look very bare, but plants, animals, and people have **adapted** to living there. We will find out how living things survive in the deserts. We will also see what is in store for the deserts of the world.

Deserts of the World

Coastal deserts and cold, dry winds

All deserts lie in areas of the world where there is very little rain. Look at the world map below. All the deserts are on huge masses of land called continents. Many deserts are located on the western side of the continents. The western side is dry because winds blowing from the west sweep across cold oceans. The coldness keeps the air from holding moisture that forms rain clouds. No rain forms, so these western coasts remain dry.

This map shows some of the world's largest deserts. Not all deserts are hot. Some deserts are cold or cool. The Gobi Desert in Asia stretches along a high, flat **plateau.** The high **altitude** makes the air very cold. The Namib Desert in southwest Africa is cooled by a cold ocean **current** that runs along the coast.

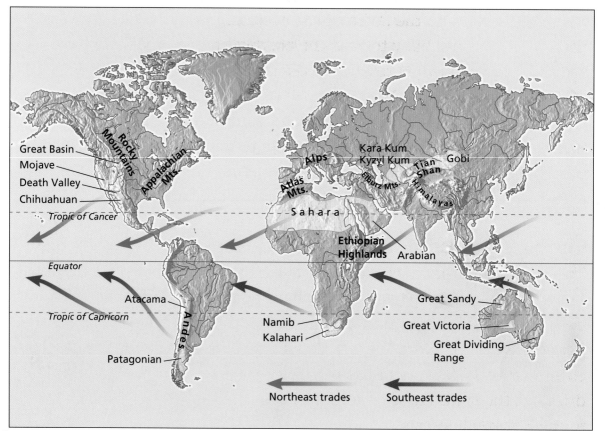

Dry rain shadow areas

Some of the deserts lie to the west of huge mountain ranges. The Andes in South America, the Rockies in North America, and the Great Dividing Range in Australia are examples of these huge ranges. The deserts to the west of them are sheltered from the constant winds that bring rain clouds. To the north of the **equator**, these winds always blow toward the northwest. To the south of the equator, they blow toward the southwest. As these winds cross the mountain ranges, they become colder and the **water vapor** in the winds cools and falls as rain. By the time the winds have crossed the mountain ranges, the air is very dry.

Tropical deserts

The map shows that many deserts are up to 1,000 miles (1,500 kilometers) north and south of the equator. These areas are known as the **Tropics**. In parts of the Tropics, the skies are clear, with very few rain clouds. The hot sun dries out the land. These conditions have formed tropical deserts.

The Mojave Desert is in California. This desert is sheltered all around by mountains. It gets very little rain. The desert is hot, but some of the higher, surrounding mountain peaks are covered in snow.

7

Desert Landscapes

Desert types

Deserts have many rocks in unusual shapes and sand **dunes** that look like huge waves. These are some of the features that make up the three main types of desert landscape—rocky, sandy, and stony. Rocky deserts are known as **hamada**. Sandy deserts are called **erg**. Stony deserts are known as **reg**. These names are from the Arabic language.

Two main factors make each desert different. The first is the type of rock that makes up the desert. Some crystal-like rocks break into sand. Harder rocks break into stones and large pieces of rock. Soft rocks wear down, first becoming hills and then becoming low-lying **plains**.

The second factor that makes different desert types is the force of sudden rain and winds that change the deserts through **erosion**.

Hot deserts can have a thin dark surface layer called desert varnish. It is made from iron deposits. In many places there is also a fine crust of plant roots. Flowers burst from these plants when it rains. These top layers keep the wind from eroding the desert. If they are destroyed, it can take the desert thousands of years to recover.

Weakened rocks

Water is important in shaping a desert. When it rains, the chemicals in the water weaken desert rock, and the rock wears away more easily. Rainwater has **minerals** and **acids** that change the chemicals in the rocks. They make the rocks crumbly. Dew that forms on the rocks at night crumbles the rock, too. So does moisture that gets sucked up from the ground. This type of action that weakens the rocks is called chemical **weathering**.

Physical weathering processes then take over. In hot deserts, the sun's heat and the night's freezing temperatures weaken rocks and stones even further. The sun beats down on the rocks during the day. This makes them expand. At night, the skies are clear and the ground is unprotected by clouds. Cold, crisp night air quickly cools the rocks and stones. This makes them shrink and crack. Water that gathers in the small cracks in the rocks freezes at night. The water expands, gradually pushing the cracks further apart. Over time, the rocks become weakened, leaving them open to the forces of the rainstorms and high winds.

This isn't really a river in the sand. It is only a **mirage**. Mirages form where layers of air with different temperatures meet. In hot deserts the air near the ground becomes hotter than the air above it, forming layers of air. Rays of sunlight beaming down on the air layers are bent, causing a mirage.

Shaped by the Rain

When rainstorms hit the hard, bare surfaces of rocky deserts, flash floods sweep through the dry landscape. There is no soil to soak up the rain. There are no plants to protect the rock surface. Raindrops batter bare rocks and stones, wearing them away. Rain collects in streams called **rivulets**. The rivulets make grooves in the land called **gullies**. The rivulets also carry small, gritty particles that scrape at the surface and make the gullies deeper.

When streams gather at the bottoms of rocky hills, they carve gigantic **canyons** or **gorges**. The canyons and gorges divide high, flat **plateaus**. Those with flat tops and steep sides are called **mesas**. Smaller steep-sided, flat-topped hills are known as **buttes**. Single mountains, called **inselbergs**, also get separated from the plateau by the gorge. After a long time, soft mountains might be worn down into a low-lying **plain**. Sometimes there is a shallow slope where the bottoms of the cliffs meet the plain.

◈ Monument Valley in Arizona and Utah is a spectacular desert landscape. Its amazing shapes have mostly been made by water **erosion**. There are humped cone hills as far as the eye can see. There are ridges, gullies, canyons, and **spires**, too. This dry desert landscape is made of layers of soft, **sedimentary** rock. When this rock is eroded by rainstorms, the layers help to make these unusual shapes. Rain also exposes the different colors of the layers.

The Great Fish River is in southwest Africa. It is normally dry, but when there is sudden rain, the wadi is filled with water. The river is then 325 feet (100 meters) wide and 30 feet (9 meters) deep.

Rivers in the sand

Heavy rain makes sudden rivers that cut deeply into sandy and stony deserts. The water carries sand or gravel, which scours the river beds and makes them deeper. When the rain stops, the rivers dry up quickly, leaving dry river beds, called **wadis**. It is thought that many of the wadis in the Sahara and Arabian Deserts were rivers at one time, when the **climate** of these regions was much wetter.

The levels of rainfall at Eismitte, Greenland, and Bahrain, on the edge of the Arabian Desert, are similar, but their temperatures are very different.

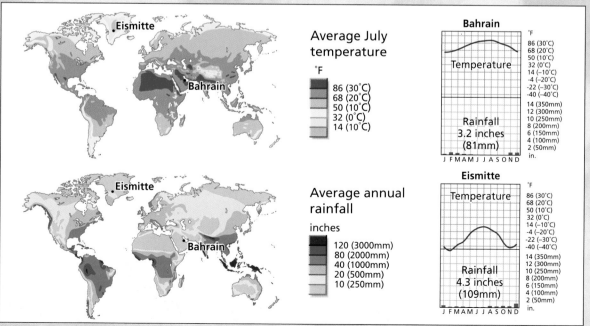

Average July temperature

°F
86 (30°C)
68 (20°C)
50 (10°C)
32 (0°C)
14 (10°C)

Average annual rainfall

inches
120 (3000mm)
80 (2000mm)
40 (1000mm)
20 (500mm)
10 (250mm)

Bahrain

°F
86 (30°C)
68 (20°C)
50 (10°C)
32 (0°C)
14 (−10°C)
−4 (−20°C)
−22 (−30°C)
−40 (−40°C)

Temperature

14 (350mm)
12 (300mm)
10 (250mm)
8 (200mm)
6 (150mm)
4 (100mm)
2 (50mm)
in.

Rainfall
3.2 inches
(81mm)

J F M A M J J A S O N D

Eismitte

°F
86 (30°C)
68 (20°C)
50 (10°C)
32 (0°C)
14 (−10°C)
−4 (−20°C)
−22 (−30°C)
−40 (−40°C)

Temperature

14 (350mm)
12 (300mm)
10 (250mm)
8 (200mm)
6 (150mm)
4 (100mm)
2 (50mm)
in.

Rainfall
4.3 inches
(109mm)

J F M A M J J A S O N D

Shaped by the Wind

Desert landscapes are also shaped by fierce desert winds. The winds bring small particles of sand and stone. The particles bounce along the ground and hit solid rocks, chipping and wearing them away. This type of **erosion** is called **abrasion**.

Wind and sand can wear away the bottoms of tall rocks to make mushroom shapes called **pedestals**. They can make ridges and furrows in the rock, known as **yardangs** and **zeugens**. They can also make flat rock surfaces with sharp edges. Sand in the wind polishes the rock faces, making them smooth and shiny.

Wind-blown shapes are really quite small. Most of the big features, such as **plains** and **plateaus,** were made by rain. But there is one large feature that is eroded by wind.

The Rub al-Khali, located mostly in Saudi Arabia, is one of the hottest sandy deserts in the world. It is also known as the Empty Quarter, because it is so hard for living things to survive there. The desert covers about 250,000 sq. mi. (650,000 sq km) and is linked to other sandy and rocky deserts in the region. Some of the huge **dunes** in the Rub al-Khali have hardened into layers of sandstone. The layers show that the wind blew in one direction.

12

This is the deflation hollow, which is a huge, scoured-out **basin**. The rock was probably first weakened and crumbled by chemical **weathering.** The wind then blew away the fragile surface. The Qattara Depression is a deflation hollow that lies in western Egypt. It is about 430 feet (130 meters) below sea level and is hundreds of miles wide.

Heaps of sand

Winds also blow sandy deserts into dunes. Some dunes have peaks as high as 650 feet (200 meters). Other dunes are shaped by the wind into crescent-shaped **barchans**, and snakelike **seifs**. These formations are caused by a strong wind blowing in just one direction. The wind pushes more sand over and around the shapes. This makes the shapes move across the desert. Star shapes are formed when the wind swirls in different directions.

In Saudi Arabia, sand dunes move an average of 48 feet (14.6 meters) each year. They clog pipelines that carry petroleum oil from oil wells to the country's **refineries**. Barriers have been built and trees have been planted to try and stop this. In the cold deserts of Antarctica, the cold winds sweep snow and ice into deep, dune-like drifts.

Pedestal formations like this occur because their rocks lie in horizontal soft and hard layers of rock. Wind erosion wears away the soft layers, leaving the shape of the hard layers towering above the ground. Yardangs and zeugens form in the same way.

Water in the Desert

Without water, there would be no spectacular desert landscapes. But most importantly, without water there would be no life in the deserts at all. Water in the desert comes in three main forms. It comes as night dew that clings to rocks and stones, as moisture that gets sucked up from the ground, and as rare rainstorms. Sometimes there are very light rainshowers as well.

Running rivers and cool oases

Sudden rain in the desert causes rivers to flow for a short while along normally dry river beds. Sometimes the rain causes flooding, which brings life to the desert.

A natural **oasis** occurs when water rises at the point where impermeable rocks curve up toward the surface of the desert. Artificial oases are made by drilling a well to the water table. Some wells are more than 3,200 feet (1,000 meters) deep. There are large cities along the north African coast, where water is plentiful, but the few settlements in the Sahara Desert are around oases.

14

In some deserts, rain runs down mountain ranges, such as the Atlas Mountains on the northern edge of the Sahara. The rainwater then flows underground. Where these underground rivers rise to the surface, they make cool, damp areas known as oases.

At other times, the water collects underground between layers of **impermeable** rock, shaped in a **basin**. The water cannot soak through the rock, so it comes to rests in these basins, forming underground lakes known as artesian basins. When wells are drilled through the rock, the pressure is so great that the water spurts up.

Salt lakes

Rivers caused by sudden rainstorms can carry rocks and stones along with them. Some desert rocks contain salt and **minerals**. When the rivers stop, the rocks and stones are left behind. These form rocky slopes called **bajadas**. The slopes get **eroded** into basins that fill with water the next time there is sudden rain. When this new lake dries up, its surface will be covered with a layer of glistening salt that comes from the rocks.

Palms and crops grow well in shady, damp oases like this one in Morocco.

Plants of the Desert

Coping in the desert

Plants in the world's deserts cope with dry conditions and rapid changes in temperature. Some plants have **adapted** themselves over thousands of years. Other plants lie **dormant,** only coming to life when rain falls on the bare rocks and sand. In hot deserts, dry seeds can lie for years near the desert surface. When rain finally comes, a carpet of flowers covers the landscape.

Some plants have adapted to the high levels of salt and other chemicals often found in desert rock and sand. These plants are called **halophytes**. The salt is concentrated in the plants' sap and comes out through tiny holes in the leaves.

You can see from the map that the Sahara is bordered by grasslands to the south. Some deserts have no grasslands around their edges, only rocky mountains or the sea.

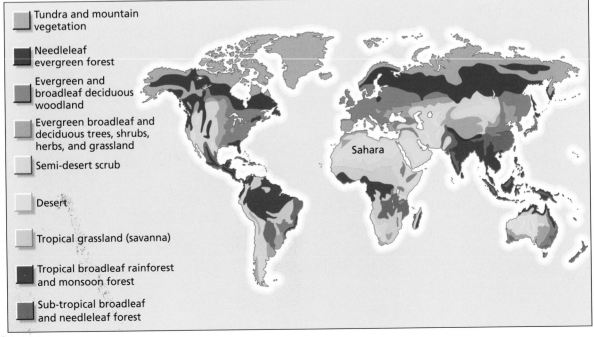

- Tundra and mountain vegetation
- Needleleaf evergreen forest
- Evergreen and broadleaf deciduous woodland
- Evergreen broadleaf and deciduous trees, shrubs, herbs, and grassland
- Semi-desert scrub
- Desert
- Tropical grassland (savanna)
- Tropical broadleaf rainforest and monsoon forest
- Sub-tropical broadleaf and needleleaf forest

Sahara

In Antarctica, there are no flowering plants at all. In the short summer, tiny mosses and **fungi** cling to small patches of bare rock. Lichens, which are a mixture of **algae** and fungi, spread a carpet of color over the rocks, too. These plants need very little water. Plants in freezing **climates** cannot suck up water through their roots like plants in hot deserts can. This is because the water is frozen into ice.

Waxy cactus

Cactuses grow mostly in the deserts of North and South America. Most have swollen stems with a waxy covering. This helps them to store water for a long time. The stems are shaped so that when water does flow, it goes directly to the roots. The huge root system spreads out far and wide. This helps the plant to absorb as much water as possible.

Some cactuses have sharp spines. These spines are their leaves. The spiny shape of the leaves helps to keep the sun and heat from drying them out. It also keeps animals from eating the cactus. Some cactuses produce beautiful flowers and soft, fleshy fruit.

The opuntia cactus comes from Central America, but it grows in many other dry regions of the world. It is used as a hedge to protect homes and animals, such as sheep. It also shelters small patches of land where crops are grown. The opuntia is also known as prickly pear because of its delicious pear-shaped fruit. In Australia the opuntia grows so well that it has become a huge, prickly weed. Millions of dollars are spent trying to get rid of it.

Desert Creatures

Adapting to the desert

Many desert mammals find shelter during the heat of the day. They are nocturnal, which means they only come out of their homes at night when it is cool. Some small mammals, such as the North American kangaroo rat and the African gerbil, are able to hold and recycle water in their bodies. They survive by eating dry seeds. Other animals, such as the horned toad, can cool their bodies by making their heart pump more slowly.

Some reptiles and amphibians sleep during very hot or dry periods. This is called **estivating.** Some amphibians, such as the Arizona spadefoot toad, bury themselves deep in the earth until it rains. Then they scramble to the surface and quickly lay their **spawn** in the newly formed puddles. By the time the puddles dry out, the young toads have grown and buried themselves underground, just like their parents.

There are no animals on the freezing land of the Antarctic, other than some tiny flies. But the coasts teem with tiny plants and sea creatures. The bodies of fish, seals, and seabirds, such as penguins, have layers of fat to help them to cope with the energy they lose in the cold.

The American southwest is the home of the roadrunner, a bird that sprints across the dry landscape to catch its prey. The lizards and snakes they catch give roadrunners enough food and liquid to survive.

18

The camel—ship of the desert

Camels are found in both hot and cold deserts. The one-humped dromedary comes from hot Arabia. The two-humped Bactrian camel comes from cool central Asia. Camels can travel long distances without food or water. For hundreds of years, desert people have used camels to carry them, their trade goods, and even their homes.

The camel's hump stores fat and flesh, which its body uses when food is scarce. A camel drinks a huge amount of water when it can, but it can survive for several days without taking any more. Water is stored in stomach pouches and released into the body when needed.

◈ Hard, **cloven** feet help the Bactrian camel grip the rocks of central Asia's deserts. Its long hair keeps out the cold.

People of the Desert

Surviving in the desert

Some desert people have survived for thousands of years by collecting enough food and water to live without disturbing the desert. They have found skillful ways of building shelters from the few bushes and trees that grow. Some make homes from hollows in cool desert mountain cliffs. The San of southern Africa, the Tuareg of north and west Africa, and the Aborigines of Australia live this way. They have also developed rich cultures that stem from their environments.

Animals are very important to the Bedouin of Arabia and north Africa. They travel across the desert on camels or horses. They also herd sheep and goats, which provide meat, milk, and wool. The wool is woven into tent material and clothing. The milk is made into cheese, or salted to keep it fresh.

On the map:

Fes
Marrakech
Tunis
Kairwan
Tripoli
MEDITERRANEAN SEA
Cairo
Nile River
Taghaza
Ghat
Marzuk
Kufra
Taoudenhi
adane
Mecca
Ghana
Tombouctou
Mali
El Fasher
Sennar

over 3000 feet (900 meters)

0   500 miles

0   500 kilometers

ert

e route

Growing food

In Saharan **oases**, cereals, fruit, vegetables, and date palms are grown. Many of these foods are dried so that they keep for a long time. This is important for people who live and travel in the desert.

For thousands of years, farmers have grown food and cotton along the banks of the Nile River in the eastern Sahara. When the Nile flooded each year, it deposited rich river soils in which to grow crops. But these soils no longer **fertilize** the valley. This is because the Aswan **Dam** collects much of the Nile's water and allows only a small amount to flow into the river. The rich, red soils now collect behind the dam. In other areas, farmers do not depend on river soils. Instead, they use water from mountain streams to **irrigate** the dry land.

Most desert people trade animals and goods, such as **minerals** and tools. Ancient trade routes have crossed the Sahara from the coasts of north Africa to the tropical forests of west Africa. Salt was an important trade item. People cannot survive in the heat without salt. Traders loaded camels with silks and gems along the Silk Road from China to Europe. This route cut across the cold, rocky deserts of central Asia.

Riches of the Desert

Deserts hold many riches. Some, such as precious stones and gold, are mined from desert rock. Petroleum oil is extracted from deep underground. In the last century, these riches have been taken from the deserts and sold throughout the world. This has made some desert countries very wealthy. It has also given people work.

In other countries, water has been brought into the desert to make farmland. **Irrigation** channels have been made and deep wells have been dug. In the **Middle East**, some of the water has been used to make golf courses. This has encouraged tourists to visit the area.

This long canal runs for 423 miles (680 kilometers) through the Thar Desert in northwest India. It was built so huge areas of desert could become farmland. Rice and other cereals, cotton, groundnuts, and oilseeds are grown. But growing crops on reclaimed deserts has its problems. The earth dries out quickly, often leaving a crusty layer of salt on the top. This crust keeps plants from growing. The process is called salinization.

Science in the desert

Antarctica is rich in **minerals**, especially oil and coal. But Antarctica is also one of the few remaining undisturbed habitats of the world. The countries of the world have agreed to use Antarctica only to set up research stations. To protect the environment, only about 1,000 scientists are allowed to live and work in Antarctica at any one time.

Oil and opals

Saudi Arabia is made up mostly of desert. Here, oil wells provide about a fourth of the world's petroleum oil each year. Underground pipelines carry oil from the oilfields to **refineries**.

Many different colored **opals** are found in South Australia. In the desert mining town of Coober Pedy, miners have made homes in the cool, empty mine holes dug into the rock.

Both hot and cold deserts have a lot of sunshine. In California, a huge solar power station traps the sun's rays and changes them into electric energy. California farmers are using solar power to pump water to their land. They are also **adapting** solar energy to build greenhouses for growing plants.

23

A Way of Life—Aborigines of Australia

Many parts of the Australian desert are semi-arid. This means that it is hot and dry most of the time. At other times, there is just enough rain for grasses, bushes, and thin, spindly trees to grow. Some lizards, kangaroos, wild camels, and birds are able to survive here. But for humans, it is very hard indeed. Aboriginal people of these deserts have learned many important skills that help them to survive. They use the features of the natural world to make a living and build a home.

Some desert homes are made from poles tied in a dome shape, then covered with bundles of **spinifex** grass. Others have straight poles with a tree-bark roof. Beds are also made of poles and raised above the ground. A fire is lit underneath to keep mosquitoes away.

Finding water

Aborigines know how to tell where underground water is by looking for clues in the landscape. They dig a deep hole and wait for muddy water to seep into it. Then they lay bunches of spinifex grass on top of the water to soak. Finally, they squeeze the water from the grass. Spinifex grass acts as a filter to make the water clear and pure.

Some trees have thick, juicy roots. Aborigines dig them up and scrape them with a flat blade. The stringy fibers are then squeezed, and water drips out.

Finding food

Aborigines gather grass seeds, bush and tree roots, and berries for food. They also eat juicy grubs and caterpillars. They use guns and spears to hunt birds, kangaroos, and lizards. The stringy **tendons** from animals' and birds' legs can be used to tie poisoned arrowheads to the spears.

Aborigines cook their food on hot stones that are placed in a hole and covered with branches.

This picture is painted on rock. It tells a traditional story. Aborigines learn desert routes through ancient songs and stories called songlines. Many of these are about animals and tell how the land was created. They are also like maps. They tell where food and water can be found.

Looking to the Future

Many of the world's deserts are getting bigger. This is known as desertification. It is caused by changes in **climate** and by human activity. In 1984 the **United Nations** made a study of desertification. The study showed that nearly a third of the earth's land is in danger of becoming desert if we are not careful.

A hotter world

In recent years, the world has been getting slightly hotter. This change is called global warming. Some scientists believe that the warming is part of a natural temperature cycle. Other scientists believe that it is because carbon dioxide and other gases are building up in the **atmosphere** around the earth. These gases trap the heat from the sun. Scientists believe that humans are

Oil wells are quite small and do not disturb the desert very much. But oil storage, pipelines, new roads to the oilfields, oil spills, transportation, and explosions cause pollution that harms the delicate desert environment.

causing this gas build-up by burning fossil fuels such as oil and coal. It is thought that flares from the sun and the position of our solar system as it moves around the galaxy are also making the earth warmer. Although not everyone agrees about what causes global warming, most people agree that it is causing desert areas to spread.

Delicate deserts

Hot deserts have a thin, delicate crust. Mining, farming, roadbuilding, and tourism damage this fragile layer. So does war. The desert environment of Kuwait was harmed by the Gulf War of 1991. Rolling tanks and burning oilfields damaged the desert crust and caused **sandstorms**.

Desert plants are special because they have **adapted** themselves to the dry conditions. But sometimes farmers burn plants on the edges of deserts to make room for crops, or they allow their animals to graze on the plants. Deserts spread when there are no natural plants left to hold the soil together. An example of this is the Sahel region on the southern edge of the Sahara.

Desert farms often use underground water from wells. This lowers the water table deep beneath the desert, which dries the desert even more. When underground desert water dries out on the farmland, it often leaves high levels of salt and other chemicals.

Desert Facts

Top ten desert regions

These are the largest deserts in the world. Some of the regions are made up of several smaller deserts. This list does not include the frozen deserts in the **polar regions**.

	Location	Area (square miles)	(square kilometers)
Sahara Desert	north Africa	3,320,000	8,600,000
Arabian Desert	southwest Asia	900,000	2,330,000
Gobi Desert	central Asia	500,000	1,300,000
Kalahari Desert	southern Africa	360,000	930,000
Patagonian Desert	Argentina	260,000	673,000
Great Victoria Desert	Australia	250,000	647,000
Great **Basin**	southwest U.S.	190,000	492,000
Chihuahuan Desert	Mexico	175,000	450,000
Great Sandy Desert	northwest Australia	150,000	400,000
Kara Kum Desert	Turkmenistan	135,000	350,000

Did you know that it can snow in hot deserts? It rarely happens, though. Snow falls when unusually strong winds blow very high up over the desert where it is extremely cold. The moisture in the air freezes and falls as snow.

Years without rain

The driest place in the world is Arica, in Chile's Atacama Desert, which has an average of .03 inches (0.8 mm) of rain every year. The longest period without rain was also in Chile, at Calama, where no rainfall was recorded until 1971.

Death Valley is a dry and often salty desert in southeast California and western Nevada. The highest recorded temperature in the United States, 134°F (56.7°C), was recorded in Death Valley in 1913. Death Valley is famous for its rich borax deposits, which were first mined more than 100 years ago. Borax is used in glassmaking and as a disinfectant.

Glossary

abrasion erosion caused by moving stones carried by wind or water

acid chemical substance that can corrode or damage other materials

adapt to change and make suitable for a new use

algae simple form of plant life, ranging from a single cell to a huge seaweed

altitude height above sea level

atmosphere layer of gases that surrounds the earth

bajada rocky slope made of stones deposited by running water

barchan crescent-shaped sand dune

basin large hollow in the land that slopes downwards, often with a river at the bottom

butte isolated hill with steep sides, formed by erosion of the rock around it

canyon narrow, steep-sided river valley

climate rainfall, temperature, and winds that normally affect a large area

cloven divided into two parts. Sheep and oxen have cloven hooves.

current water that flows constantly in one direction in an ocean

dam wall that is built across a river valley to hold back water, creating an artificial lake

dormant being temporarily in an inactive state

dune hill or ridge of sand formed by the wind that looks like a wave

equator imaginary line around the earth, exactly half way between the North and South Poles

erg sandy desert landscape

erosion wearing away of rocks and soil by wind, water, ice, or acid

estivate to sleep during very hot or dry periods

fertile describes rich soil in which crops can grow easily

fungus (more than one are called fungi) simple plant, such as a mold or mushroom, that lives off of other plants, animals, or decaying material

gorge narrow passage, often between two mountains

gully groove worn into the earth by rivulets

halophyte plant that can cope with salty growing conditions

hamada rocky desert landscape

impermeable not allowing water to pass through

inselberg single mountain left behind after surrounding mountains have eroded away

irrigate to supply a place or area with water, for example to grow crops

mesa flat-topped hill separated from a plateau by erosion

Middle East area between the eastern Mediterranean and India, particularly Israel and the Arab countries

mineral substance formed naturally in rock or earth, such as oil or salt

mirage optical illusion caused by light being bent through layers of warm air near the ground

oasis area of wet, fertile land in the middle of a desert

opal whitish gem with streaks of changeable color

pedestal mushroom-shaped rock shaped by wind erosion

plain area of flat land or low-lying hills

plateau area of high, flat ground, often lying between mountains

polar region area around the North or South Pole

refinery factory where a raw material, such as oil, is changed into one that can be more easily used

reg stony desert landscape

rivulet small stream

sandstorm storm in which the wind drives clouds of sand across a desert

sedimentary soft type of rock formed from soil and rock deposited by wind or water

seif long, narrow sand dune

tendon strong, stringy fiber that connects a muscle to a bone

spawn egg cells produced by amphibians

spinifex type of grass found in Australia, with stiff, sharp leaves

spire something that is very tall, thin and pointed at the top

Tropics region between the Tropic of Cancer and the Tropic of Capricorn, two imaginary lines that circle the earth above and below the equator.

United Nations organization that tries to solve international problems and protect human rights

wadi dry river bed

water vapor water that has been heated so much that it forms a gas that is held in the air

weathering action of weather on rock or other materials

yardang ridge formed by wind erosion

zeugen flat-topped ridge formed by wind erosion

More Books to Read

Jenkins, Martin. *Deserts*. Minneapolis: The Lerner Publishing Group, 1996.

Lambert, David. *People of the Deserts*. Austin, Tex.: Raintree Steck-Vaughn, 1999.

Sanders, John. *All about Deserts*. Mahwah, N.J.: Troll Communications, 1997.

Savage, Stephen. *Animals of the Desert*. Austin, Tex.: Raintree Steck-Vaughn, 1997.

Taylor, Barbara. *Desert Life*. New York: DK Publishing, Inc., 1998.

Index